Sages, Smart Alecks, and Schlemiels

New and Selected Poems

Robert H. Deluty

PHOENICIA, NEW YORK 2024

Copyright © 2024 by
Robert H. Deluty
All rights reserved.

Permission to reproduce in any form
must be secured from the author.

Please direct all correspondence to
Robert H. Deluty's email address:
deluty@umbc.edu

Library of Congress Control Number 2024911036
ISBN: 978-0-9851283-0-2

Published by

Heron Creek Press, LLC
P.O. Box 207
Phoenicia, NY 12464

www.heroncreekpress.com

Printed in the United States of America

To

Erika Berenguer Gil

Contents

One Morning at Montessori 1

Insight 2

Psychology 101 3

Winning the Argument 4

Role Model 5

Reality 6

Keeping it Respectable 7

School Assembly 8

Senryu 9

Senryu 10

Senryu 11

Senryu 12

Left End of the Bell Curve 13

Nineteen Years Later 14

States of the Game 15

Too Long in Academia 16

Posthumous 17

Loud and Clear 18

Emergency Room Visit 19

The Linguist 20

English Department 21

Senryu 22

Senryu 23

Senryu 24

Senryu 25

Senryu 26

Senryu 27

Sophomore 28

In the Elevator 29

Rest in Peace 30

The Professional 31

Mementos 32

Past/Present 33

Senryu 34

Senryu 35

Senryu 36

Senryu 37

Senryu 38

Revelation 39

To Your Health................................... 40

Feedback 41

The Bottom Line................................ 42

Antidote.. 43

Honest to a Fault................................ 44

On the Road to Immortality 45

She's a Keeper..................................... 46

Grateful... 47

Wisenheimers...................................... 48

Genius, Ignorance 49

Quality Time...................................... 50

Planning Ahead.................................. 51

Making the Best of It......................... 52

Truth Serum....................................... 53

Begorra.. 54

Rejoinder 55

Taking on the World 56

Higher Education............................... 57

Low Finance....................................... 58

A Splendid Start 59

At Children's Hospital 60

God Bless the Americas 61

Father Knows Best 62

Constructive Criticism 63

Punctuation 64

The Connoisseur 65

Wonderland 66

Abnormal Psychology 67

About the author 69

One Morning at Montessori

The teacher announces that

The letter of the day is *k*.

Explaining that *k* words

Have the *kuh* sound,

She asks for examples.

One child shouts *cat*.

A second offers *carrot*.

A third, *cotton*.

The teacher explains that

All of these *kuh* words

Begin with a *c*.

Sensing the children's confusion,

She asks her student teacher

For a *k* word.

Knife, he replies.

Insight

Asked what

His mother and father

Have in common,

The third grader

Thinks long and hard

Before answering

With dead seriousness

And utmost certitude,

Neither one wants

Another kid

Psychology 101

For the final exam in Intro Psych,
A young professor gives her students
Three hours to answer one hundred questions.
About fifty percent finish within one hour,
Ninety percent within two.
Thirty minutes later, only one student remains.
He continues to pore over the exam
For the next half-hour, stopping only after
The professor impatiently announces time's up.
The student, named Kreppel,
Achieves the only perfect score.

Twenty-four years later, the same professor
Gives her Intro Psych class a final exam
Of one hundred questions. Once again,
Only one student takes all three hours
To complete the exam – the only one
To achieve a perfect score.
Kreppel's daughter.

Winning the Argument

After giggling, clowning,

Burping, screeching, mugging,

Pratfalling, eye-crossing and

Knock-knock joking

All weekend long,

The seven-year-old comedian's

Exasperated mother screams,

No one finds you funny!

To which her son replies,

My girlfriend does.

Role Model

The renowned professor
Of electrical engineering
Explains to his students
Why he doesn't own a PC:
I'm either in a meeting,
The library, a classroom,
My office or my lab
From 8:00 a.m. to 10 p.m.
Seven days a week.
I go to my apartment
To shower and sleep.
Why on earth would I need
A home computer?

Reality

Moms and Dads have heard
well-meaning friends, teachers,
and television characters
preaching to their children that
they can be anything they want to be
as long as they are passionate,
as long as they give it their all,
as long as they believe in themselves.

But – for the mentally retarded boy
who dreams of being a surgeon;
for the short, clumsy adolescent
longing to be an Olympic athlete;
for the child with palsy who aspires
to be a star of stage and screen –
their parents know better.

Keeping it Respectable

Asked by his six year-old

Why men and women sit separately

In their Orthodox synagogue,

A father replies that, because

The rabbi's sermons are so dull,

People tend to nod off;

And it would not be proper

For male and female adults

In a house of worship

To sleep together

School Assembly

The United States Poet Laureate
Agrees to visit the elementary school
He attended fifty years earlier, and to
Give a lecture to all 3rd – 5th graders.
After discussing sonnets, free verse,
Quatrains, senryu, limericks,
Villanelles and haibun,
And reciting for thirty minutes
His own award-winning poetry,
He asks the children if they have any questions.

I do, I do, exclaims a fourth grader
Sitting in the second row.
How much wood would a woodchuck chuck
If a woodchuck could chuck wood?

Senryu

centenarian
still calling her eldest child
a work in progress

Nobel scientist
drawing a blank when asked
for his zip code

telling her grandson
to be kind and gracious
or she'll smack him

mid-thunderstorm . . .
TV weatherman proclaims
there's a chance of rain

the elder claiming
the far greater Costello
was Lou, not Elvis

Senryu

the wordsmith noting
Geraldine is *realigned*
realigned

in Sunday School,
an eight year-old questioning
how much Moses weighed

her teen explaining
why fame is more important
than decency

asked what do you call
having just one spouse, Dad states
Monotony

advising his niece,
battling profound hopelessness,
Others have it worse

Senryu

biblical scholar
characterizing *thou*
as *the old you*

mini-golf course . . .
nine-year-old twins inquiring
could they be caddies

while meditating,
Grandpa thinking of folks
who owe him money

Methodist lawyer
calling Alan Dershowitz
a real schmuck

Quaker columnist
deeming Ben Shapiro
a total putz

Senryu

computer salesman
claiming he graduated
from Harvard Tech

tractor repairman
boasting he studied
at Yale A&M

their son-in-law
taking *You are shameless*
as a compliment

a preteen
scowling that *forever stamps*
can be used just once

her student noting
he hates grammar, but can
tolerate usage

Left End of the Bell Curve

After performing abysmally

On a test requiring students

To name and locate

The world's continents,

A fifth grader approaches

His teacher and explains that

He has never set foot

Outside of New Jersey and,

To make matters worse,

He's got a learning disability

When it comes to geometry

Nineteen Years Later

At the supermarket,

The retired college counselor

Runs into a former student

Named Bethany who came to see him

Only once – when she threatened suicide

Believing she had failed her Econ I final.

Bethany thanks him profusely, noting

That his kindness, wisdom, and perspective

Might well have saved her life that day.

After accepting her gratitude and

Exchanging pleasantries, the counselor inquires

About the grade she received on the exam.

I was afraid you'd ask, she replies. *I got an A.*

States of the Game

Looks at Michigan,

sees a catcher's mitt.

At Colorado and Wyoming,

first and second base.

Nevada, home plate.

Tennessee, base path.

Florida, broken bat.

[Delaware and New Jersey,

slivers of that bat.]

Baseball fever rages

in geography class.

Too Long in Academia

Put her latest effort in

A colleague's mailbox.

Thanks for your memo,

He noted later.

It's called a poem,

She replied.

Posthumous

Every night

alone in bed

he imagines the days

following his death.

He sees weeping relatives

extolling his talents and promise.

Broken-hearted ex-girlfriends

bemoaning their lost opportunities.

Guilt-ridden co-workers

wishing they had shown him

kindness and respect.

His pastor, ashen and trembling,

expressing the community's anguish.

Every night

he imagines these scenes,

then drifts off to sleep

Smiling.

Loud and Clear

Organic chemistry final exam.

In an ocean of panic, despair,

Solemnity and silence,

A freshman's cell phone goes off,

Fracturing the class with a ring tone:

I can't get no . . . satisfaction.

Emergency Room Visit

Her octogenarian father –

Remarkably fit, handsome,

Stubborn and vain –

Drives himself to the hospital

Convinced he has pneumonia.

After turning in his paperwork,

He overhears two nurses

Whispering that he looks

More like 62 than 82.

Deeply offended,

He roars at them,

When I'm not sick,

I look 42!

The Linguist

Getting dressed one morning,

Their nine-year-old grandson

Reasons if briefs and boxers

Are termed *underwear,* and

Raincoats and windbreakers

Are considered *outerwear,*

Then shirts and pants

Must be *wear*

English Department

During the orientation of
First-year graduate students,
After all of his colleagues have
Introduced themselves and
Described their current research,
The department's eldest professor,
An eminent Shakespearean scholar,
Takes the floor and declares,
I'm a joker, I'm a smoker,
I'm a midnight toker . . . .

Senryu

ticketed driver
telling the speeding cop
he's a hypocrite

the Nobel winner
sobbing that her parents died
in their forties

upscale coffee shop . . .
an elderly man asking
if *Sanka* is served

father of three sons
boasting of the achievements
only of his dog

intending
to compliment her dimples,
the priest says *Nipples*

Senryu

game night . . .
the sign language instructor
cheating at charades

recommending
his wife use a pet name
besides *Imbecile*

begging the stranger
in the other men's room stall
to stop yodeling

a young poet
hoping never to be called
accessible

refusing to grant
her mate's wish to be buried
in his bowling shirt

Senryu

deeply regretting
asking the obese woman
when she is due

on a dare
belting out *I Feel Pretty*
in a redneck bar

asked to describe
his wife of thirty years,
he says *Left-handed*

asked to describe
her husband of thirty years,
she replies *Pissed off*

a five-year-old girl
announcing she's most grateful
for *Mom, Dad, fingers*

Senryu

a hapless thief
stealing the identity
of a wanted man

two philosophers
confessing their shared love
of Curly Howard

a personal best . . .
their mother taking home
nine *Hilton* towels

Valentine miscue . . .
his new girlfriend rejecting
the heart-shaped thong

twelve hundred pages . . .
first-time novelist argues
nothing can be pared

Senryu

the neo-Nazi
learning too late Rabbi Katz
holds a black belt

her brother-in-law
selecting tattooed muscles
for his flabby arms

roaring with laughter
after his wife proclaims
she envies no one

two jocks discussing
would their SATs improve
on steroids

a professor
raising his voice as he speaks
to a blind student

Senryu

asking the psychic
which marriage counselor
she'd recommend

the alum showing
his sons the library nooks
where he slept

their teen promising
to change her car's oil every
fifty thousand miles

a white Brandeis prof
asserting Sammy Davis
wasn't black enough

his mother-in-law
trying to sell a cheese puff
resembling Ted Cruz

Sophomore

Arriving late

For a make-up exam,

She breathlessly offers

Her apologies to the professor,

Noting that she hopes

Her actions have not

Resulted in any

Incontinence

In the Elevator

The college provost

Overhears a snippet

Of conversation

Between two undergrads –

She's not the beautifullest girl

But she's not an ugger neither,

Just kinda, ya know . . .

Crap, I'm late for my final –

And returns to his office,

Fearing for the future

Rest in Peace

At the funeral of her older brother
She does not think about
> His jealousy, sarcasm, and rage
>
> His refusing to come to her wedding
>
> His coldness towards her children
>
> His not returning her phone calls and letters
>
> His blaming her for all his failures.

Instead, she focuses on the night
He stayed up until 3:00 a.m.
Writing a book report for her
While she slept soundly
Fifty-two years ago.

The Professional

To his bitter, whining

Long-term patient,

The psychologist edits out

Oy!

Grow up!

Knock it off!

You're killing me!

Stop complaining already!

Say something I haven't heard!

*What do you want **me** to do about it?*

*What role do **you** play in your misfortune?*

And, instead, offers

Tell me more.

Mementos

Three days after his mother's passing,

he finds in her Brooklyn apartment,

among financial files and family photos,

a folder labeled *Ben's Achievements*.

Within it, in consecutive order, he discovers

his high school valedictory address,

his college and medical school acceptance letters,

the announcements of his Dean's List

and Phi Beta Kappa inductions, and

his Certificate of Circumcision.

Past/Present

Born out of wedlock in Panama,
Raised in wretched poverty,
She was permitted one-quarter of
One page of a discarded newspaper
When she needed to go to
The communal outhouse.

Four decades later,
Now the wife of an oil company titan,
She finds herself in a five-star restaurant
Gently explaining to a young waiter
Why she needs a spoon, not a fork,
For her tiramisu.

Senryu

Nobel winner's Mom
telling the news reporters
his sister's smarter

a high-priced lawyer
defending the thief who steals
only stop signs

Yeshiva student
searching for a loophole
concerning shellfish

family elder
noting why the good old days
were miserable

his son composing
a concerto for trombone
and tugboat whistle

Senryu

Mom and Pop
questioning his investment
in *Finkelstein's Bar*

English professor
pinching the colleague who said
Very unique

asked what he's up to,
their ten year-old responding
My neck in trouble

her son's term paper . . .
a typed zero wherever
an o should be

his Idaho wife
referring to dreidels
as *New York tops*

Senryu

claiming the wisdom
of her hair stylist exceeds
that of her shrink

eve of the trial . . .
asking his attorney
to lend him socks

the college freshman
bragging that his memory
is *phonographic*

her estranged sister
coming to the funeral
in leopard pants

an elder
urging the hungry child
to whistle

Senryu

the esteemed linguist
purposely mispronouncing
his rivals' names

taking great pleasure
informing her vain husband
peacocks are males

guilty as sin,
counting on her cleavage
to sway one juror

three geographers
debating which state would make
the coolest last name

a Princeton senior
asking his Mom how to write
a Q in cursive

Senryu

explaining
why she only dates guys
whose parents are dead

Texas barbeque . . .
his vegan grandchild eating
nothing but relish

misinterpreting
the broken middle finger
of an employee

their first grader
inventing a letter
between I and J

a mother bragging
she can't fathom one sentence
of her son's thesis

Revelation

In the midst of a faculty meeting

so dull it is physically painful,

a wise guy realizes that

the letters of

ROBERT H DELUTY

can be rearranged to create

THE TRULY BORED and

TRULY BOTHERED

To Your Health

Martini olives,

Gibson pearl onions,

Bloody Mary celery stalks,

Orange zests, lime wedges,

Maraschino cherries,

Hard apple cider,

Peach schnapps,

Apricot brandy,

Banana daiquiris,

Slivovitz and Limoncello.

Her grandfather's answer to
Have you been eating your
Fruits and vegetables?

Feedback

Informing

The faculty colleague –

Who opened his latest book

And asserted that the poems

Were bizarre, disjointed and

Utterly incomprehensible –

That she had been reading

The Table of Contents

The Bottom Line

After spending fifty minutes

Discussing distinctions

In the education,

Clinical training,

Research experiences,

Roles, competencies and

Responsibilities of

Psychologists, psychiatrists, social workers,

Psychoanalysts, psychiatric nurses,

Marriage counselors, and family therapists,

A student in the front row inquires

Who makes the most?

Antidote

Whenever depression strikes,

She removes from her wallet

A forty-year-old photograph

Of her conservative father as a

Chubby, acne-covered teen

At his high school prom

Sporting a wide, goofy grin,

Shoulder-length hair, sideburns,

Braces, black horn-rimmed glasses,

A polka dot bowtie and

An eggshell-blue tuxedo

Honest to a Fault

The old chemistry professor
Explains to his young colleague
Why he so despises
Committee meetings:
They prevent me from doing
What I love the most and
Do the best –
Sitting in my lab,
In peace and quiet,
Playing solitaire

On the Road to Immortality

A high school physics student,

Dreaming of a Harvard Ph.D.,

An endowed professorship,

A Nobel Prize, and of joining

Newton, Gauss, Curie,

Joule, Tesla, Weber, Ohm,

Hertz, Kelvin, Coulomb,

Maxwell, Gray, Pascal,

Planck, Volta, and Watt

With eponyms in their honor,

Fears it will never happen

As he was cursed with

The last name Schmuckler

She's a Keeper

In a Boston bar,

His beautiful blind date

Points to the television

Airing an opening-round

World Cup soccer match

Between Norway and

Equatorial Guinea,

And inquires

Which team is which?

Grateful

After spending

A delightful afternoon

With his adoring, angelic

Three- and five-year-old

Granddaughters, he

Thanks God for granting him

The wisdom and restraint

Two decades earlier

Not to strangle their father

Wisenheimers

In response

To his query

Regarding in which dress

They should bury

Their late mother,

His sons declare

It should be

The black one,

Because they intend

To bury him

In the blue one

Genius, Ignorance

The child of an

Auschwitz survivor

Wishing he could

Ride in a Ford;

Look at a Renoir, a Degas;

Listen to Chopin, Tchaikovsky,

Wagner, Strauss, Theodorakis; and

Read Chaucer, Marlowe, Voltaire,

Kant, Gogol, Dostoevsky, Dreiser,

Pound, Eliot, Dahl, Hemingway

Without thinking

Anti-Semitic bastard

Quality Time

Over dinner,

Listening to his engineer Dad

And child psychologist Mom

Talking shop,

Their thirteen-year-old son

Ponders which

Is more unbearable:

Technospeak or

Psychobabble

Planning Ahead

After going bowling

With his father,

The five year-old climbs into

Their SUV and sits down on

His older sister's booster seat.

When asked why, he replies

He forgot to go to the bathroom,

So in case he has to pee

Before reaching home,

He doesn't want to ruin

His own seat.

Making the Best of It

A Tufts freshman,

Utterly unprepared

To give his oral presentation

In Elementary French,

Decides to deliver an

Extemporaneous address

To his classmates and professor

In Pepé Le Pew-accented English

Truth Serum

Asked why he accepted

The ultra-demanding new job,

Their father explains that

His three interviewers,

Over dinner and drinks,

Got utterly plastered,

Yet

With their inhibitions,

Defenses and filters

At their lowest, they

Spoke only positively

About their colleagues

And management

Begorra

Every year

On the seventeenth of March

Isaac Zsigmond Oberlander,

A Jewish nonagenarian

Born and raised in Hungary,

Dresses in green,

Adopts a brogue, and

Signs his last name with

An apostrophe and

A capital *B*

Rejoinder

The psychology professor,

Hearing from the editor of

The top-tier journal that

His rejected manuscript was

Peer-reviewed by

Three noted scholars,

Responds with

A four-word email:

I have no peers

Taking on the World

After doing extensive

Internet and library research,

Their eighth grader announces

That, before he dies,

He wants to visit

Poo, India

Brest, France

Crap, Albania

Seymen, Turkey

Climax, Colorado

Hooker, Oklahoma

Lake Titicaca, Peru

Middelfart, Denmark

Spread Eagle, Wisconsin

Intercourse Pennsylvania &

Horneytown, North Carolina

Higher Education

After explaining to his class
The importance of proper
Spelling, grammar, usage,
Punctuation, citations, and
References when writing
Their term papers,
The professor fields
A question from a
Dead-serious sophomore:
Does content count?

Low Finance

The old woman

Enlightening

Her ten-year-old

Great-grandson

That a six-figure salary

Most certainly

Does **not** include

The two figures

To the right of

The decimal point

A Splendid Start

A freshman approaches
the Biology professor on
the first day of classes, pleading
to be allowed to register
for her course, now closed.
After explaining to him that
she cannot allow him in because
every seat is filled and
no more chairs can fit
in the room, he remarks
Oh, that won't be a problem.
I wasn't planning on coming to class.

At Children's Hospital

Listening

To the radio pitchman

Asserting *There's nothing*

Worse than a computer

That's slow and unreliable,

The eleven-year-old boy

Battling a brain tumor

And his nurse turn

To each other and

Utter in unison,

Asshole

God Bless the Americas

On the campaign trail,

A GOP candidate

From Miami-Dade County

Running for the Florida Senate

Refers to his daughter-in-law,

Born and raised

In Santo Domingo de Guzman,

As a *Dominican Republican*

Father Knows Best

The young couple and

Their six-month-old daughter

Meet the veteran photographer

Who employs every tried-and-true

Tactic to get the baby to smile.

Tickles are met with grimaces.

Squeak toys evoke tears.

Funny faces elicit blank stares.

Finally, Dad takes

The baby from Mom and

Throws her high in the air.

The infant comes down with

A joyous, open-mouthed grin,

Mom and Dad beam, and

The photographer whispers

Got it.

Constructive Criticism

The sociology professor
Is unsure whether to laugh,
Cry or scream as he reads
The end-of-semester evaluation
Written by a sophomore major:
You look exactly like the guy
Who cleans our gutters, so
I couldn't take anything
You said seriously

Punctuation

The elder

Describing

To his grandchildren

How, over time,

He has evolved

From an apostrophe

To an exclamation point

To a question mark

The Connoisseur

Asked why he finds
Fast food so appealing,
Their son responds that
The bag and wrapper
Truly make the meal.
After all, he explains,
Presentation is crucial.

Wonderland

Look at the rainbow pancake!
The little kite swims really fast!
That one's like a juice box with eyes!
Dolphins are shinier than rain boots!
Second graders become poets
Walking through the aquarium.

Abnormal Psychology

The college student

Who never asked a question nor

Participated in a discussion, and

Who received a grade of *C* or *D*

On each of her five examinations,

Class presentation, and term project,

Approaches her professor as grades

Are about to be turned in and

Pleads for a *B*, noting that she

Attended all but four lectures,

Came late only three times,

Was always courteous, and

Did most of the readings

About the author

Dr. Robert H. Deluty is Associate Dean Emeritus of the Graduate School at the University of Maryland, Baltimore County. A psychology professor at UMBC from 1980 to 2016, he was named Presidential Teaching Professor in 2002. Dr. Deluty's poems and essays have been published in *The Wall Street Journal, The Baltimore Sun, The Pegasus Review, Modern Haiku, Voices: The Art and Science of Psychotherapy, Psychiatric Times, Jewish Currents, the Journal of Poetry Therapy, Welcome Home, Muse of Fire, Maryland Family Magazine, Gastronomica: The Journal of Food and Culture, The Faculty Voice*, and many other newspapers, journals and anthologies. *Sages, Smart Alecks, and Schlemiels* is his sixty-seventh book.